PIONEERS

RAISING UP MISSIONARY DISCIPLES FOR THE NEW FRONTIER

Jon Wiest & Ed Love

Copyright

Pioneers: Raising Up Missionary Disciples for the New Frontier

© 2020

Printed in the United States of America.

ISBN: 9798615443206

Cover and layout design by Live Design.

"Forget the former things; do not dwell on the past. See, I am doing a new thing! Now it springs up; do you not perceive it? I am making a way in the wilderness and streams in the wasteland."

Isaiah 43:18–19

CONTENTS

INTRODUCTION

Born for Adventure

*Two roads diverged in a wood, and I—
I took the one less traveled by,
and that has made all the difference.*

Robert Frost

*While they were worshiping the Lord and fasting, the
Holy Spirit said, "Set apart for me Barnabas and Saul
for the work to which I have called them." So after they
had fasted and prayed, they placed their hands on
them and sent them off.*

Acts 13:2–3

Have you ever felt like you were born in the wrong era?

As one who grew up watching *Little House on the Prairie*, I
(Ed) have always thought that I would have loved to live
in the days of the frontier, as pioneers were moving into
the Wild West. The pioneering lifestyle may have been
hard but living on the edge of adventure would have
made it all worth it!

That's probably why I'm drawn to the idea of being a
frontiersman. I tend to be a bit of a thrill-seeker. I love the
rush of new experiences. If I'm not exploring or starting
something new, life can begin to feel a little dull. I enjoy a
challenge.

I suspect my thrill-seeking impulse may have been why God called me into church planting. Starting new churches provided an opportunity for my pioneering spirit to grow and thrive.

A *pioneer* is one who is the first to open or prepare a way, settlement, or region—giving others the opportunity to occupy and develop. In other words, a pioneer goes first. They are selfless, assertive, forward-thinking initiators.

A pioneering leader is the opposite of a *settler*—someone who is less adventurous, risk-averse, and better equipped to stay and maintain what seems to work than launch into new territory. I learned early on in my ministry, that maintaining the status quo isn't my calling. I need to blaze new trails.

Jon and I both sense that God is orchestrating a growing wave of pioneering leaders—spiritual entrepreneurs willing to launch hundreds and thousands of new pioneering projects.

It is our conviction that congregations everywhere are filled with an untapped kingdom force waiting to be released into ministry. These pioneering leaders simply need permission, encouragement, and trailblazing coaches to guide them into the new frontier.

We have dedicated our lives to helping churches mobilize disciple makers, church planters, and pioneering leaders—those who can create and support the groundswell of focused energy required to reach the ever-growing harvest of the 21st-century. While there are hundreds of resources available for disciple makers, and hundreds more for church planters, the role of the pioneering leader has too often been overlooked.

We believe these leaders are the missing link, the bridge between intentional disciple making and planting new churches.

We also believe pioneering leaders are perhaps the most influential people when it comes to the future formation of the church. Whether you are a pastor interested in learning more or a disciple of Christ ready to be challenged to become a missionary in your community, this book is for you.

Throughout this book, we will define pioneering leaders, explore biblical and historical examples of pioneers, and unpack the principles found in Luke 10, which will serve as a blueprint for launching pioneering projects.

If you are sensing God stirring your missionary heart but struggle to know what to do about it, then these pages are for you.

Let's go . . .

1

THE PIONEERING LEADER

The mass of people lead lives of quiet desperation.

Henry David Thoreau

So, Abram went, as the LORD had told him...

Genesis 12:4a

In sports and every area of my life, I (Ed) seemed to be a pretty unremarkable kid. Eventually, I accepted the fact that I was just an average Joe.

When I recommitted my life to Christ, however, I was shocked to discover that God doesn't function like grade-school kickball team captains. He doesn't size up his children and select the strongest first. In a bizarre way, God often uses the weak links—the underdogs—for his kingdom work.

I can still remember the moment, at the age of 18, when I sensed the Lord calling me to dedicate my life to kingdom service. In the midst of a moonlit stroll down a nature trail, I prayed to God, "I'm finally ready to repent of my self-centered ways and I want to surrender to your will. I'll do whatever you ask of me."

Instantly, the Holy Spirit spoke to the deepest part of my heart with these three words: build – my – church.

I wish I could say my response was filled with trust and obedience, but in all honesty, it went something like this: "Build your church? Whoa. Hold on God. I said I was willing to do whatever, but I didn't really mean *whatever*. I'm definitely not a preacher, pastor, or leader-type person. You know me. I'm the shy guy. I'm an introvert. I hate public speaking. I'm not very smart. I'm not good at anything. I'm certainly not a person of influence. You've got the wrong guy. Seriously, God, I'm pretty sure I can't do what you're asking."

I waited a few moments for some sort of response. I don't know what I was expecting. Maybe I was hoping God would make a case for me. He didn't. God was silent.

My first reaction when I sensed God nudging me to dedicate my life to catalyzing his church was to ask, "Who am I, God?" I didn't seem to have any great natural leadership abilities, and I couldn't picture how the Lord might be able to use me in his purposes.

For weeks, I wrestled with myself and my greatest fears. From a human perspective, this outlandish ask from God didn't make sense at all. I genuinely wondered if God had his wires crossed. I just did not fit the church leader mold—and I certainly had no desire to be like the oddball preacher on *The Simpsons*. Never in a thousand years could I envision myself leading God's people, and I suspected my friends and family would agree!

Nevertheless, I finally submitted to my heavenly Father. In a quiet moment I prayed, "I really don't know how your plans are going to come together, but I will trust you." Immediately, I felt a peace I had never experienced before in my life. I knew I was on the right track. Yet I also started to wonder how I was going to overcome some of my greatest fears.

One day, as I was exploring the Scriptures, I came across an interesting story in Acts 4, where Peter and John were preaching and eventually arrested for creating a civil disruption. Apparently, some leaders within the Jewish religion didn't appreciate their message or tactics.

After their arrest, Peter and John were required to appear before the Jewish court of law. In the middle of their trial, Peter, filled with the Holy Spirit, stood up and shared the salvation message. The leaders couldn't believe what they were witnessing. The passage says, "When they saw the courage of Peter and John and realized that they were unschooled, ordinary men, they were astonished and they took note that these men had been with Jesus" (Acts 4:13).

This little story grabbed my attention in a big way. God used two ordinary people to do something extraordinary. Peter and John would not have been first-round draft picks. They were average Joes. Two of the most influential disciples of Jesus were run of the mill! This made me wonder even more about my life. If Peter and John were considered average and ordinary, then maybe God could use me after all. Maybe I could become one of his pioneering leaders!

Most of us understand what is meant by the terms *disciple* and *disciple maker*, but the phrase *pioneering leader* might be less familiar. While the specific phrase isn't used in the Bible, the examples of pioneering leaders are radiating throughout its pages.

Pioneering leaders are men and women willing to step out in faith in the face of uncertainty. They don't know all the details about the way forward, but they are willing to step out and risk, forging new paths. They are innovators and spiritual entrepreneurs, willing to push new boundaries to advance a cause or idea. They have an apostolic bent and are willing to build relationships and bring the gospel into a new subculture, geography, or group of people.

Here is a working definition of what we mean by a pioneering leader:

> *A pioneering leader is a missionary disciple called to find creative ways to engage and serve a group of people uncomfortable or unfamiliar with the established church.*

Pioneering leaders prioritize the word *go* in the Great Commission (Matthew 28:19-20). While they understand the call of Christ is to make disciples of *all* people, they prefer to begin the process with those far from God.

Pioneering leaders are what we might call *missionary disciples*. They are found in every walk of life. They are businesspeople, teachers, homemakers, electricians, bus drivers, teachers, baristas, musicians, entrepreneurs, and any other profession you can imagine.

They meet in neighborhoods, coffee shops, workout facilities, boxing clubs, bingo halls, retirement centers, and business offices. The combinations and gathering places are endless!

The only prerequisites for their ministry are a love for God, a love for others, and a willingness to serve a group of people uncomfortable or unfamiliar with the established church. Many of these pioneering leaders serve unreached people groups around the world, while others stay closer to home.

Anywhere people gather, any activity bringing people together, and any group in need of the Good News of Jesus is where pioneering leaders thrive as they launch out and start something new.

We believe there are tens of thousands of pioneering leaders sitting in churches everywhere waiting to be activated and mobilized. Maybe you identify with this description of a pioneering leader or maybe God is bringing someone else to mind that needs to read this book!

It is not an exaggeration to say we believe pioneering leaders are the men and women most responsible for the future formation of the church.

Pioneering leaders truly are the gatekeepers in a seismic shift currently underway in our culture.

2

THE 21ˢᵗ-CENTURY FRONTIER

*If I had asked people what they wanted, they would
have said faster horses.*

Henry Ford

*See, I am doing a new thing! Now it springs up; do you
not perceive it? I am making a way in the wilderness
and streams in the wasteland.*

Isaiah 43:19

I (Jon) remember listening to my parents tell stories of
what life was like when they were kids. The stories
seemed to ramp up whenever I started complaining about
the quality of my life or the difficulties of my childhood.
I'm probably not the first one to hear some variation of
the phrase, "Son, when I was a kid, I had to walk to school
uphill both ways in ten feet of snow." You get the drift
(sorry, bad pun).

I now have four daughters of my own, and I'm the one
telling the stories. Recently, my 16-year-old was
complaining about not having access to her smartphone
in her room, and I was ready with my response: "Honey,
when I was a kid, we only had one phone in the entire
house, and it was attached to the wall with a cord. I could

never talk on the phone in my room." The story is only partly true. Our family eventually invested in a cord stretching about one-hundred feet that could reach any room in the house! Times certainly have changed.

It's strange to think the iPhone was first released less than fifteen years ago. Now, over half of the world has a smartphone in the palm of their hands. The technological advancements of the past decade have been staggering. I am regularly on HD video conference calls with pastors that can join from anywhere around the world. Even more, I can now tell my Google home device to play the blues and immediately enjoy the sound of B.B. King on the audio bar of my flat screen TV.

Things are changing at a feverish pace. The economy, technology, family structure, neighborhoods, organizations, and networks in our world are continuously shifting. In addition, we are facing the reality of an unstable religious culture in America, best described as post-Christian.

Our world is entering a new frontier, and the need for pioneers to reimagine Christianity within the 21st-century has never been greater.

Missiologist, Alan Hirsch, has suggested that only 40 to 50 percent of the American population is reachable by the predominant presentation of church as we know it. Hirsch also believes the unreachable percentages are growing.[1]

Statistics seem to back up Hirsch's argument. 80 percent of all churches in America are plateaued and declining. When it comes to the Protestant church, only 10 percent are growing through conversion growth.[2] The large majority of growth in the other churches is through transfers from one church to another. Individual churches may be growing, but kingdom growth is slowing.

The increase among those who categorize themselves as having either no religion (the nones) or who are done with the established church (the dones) make it clear we are entering a new frontier.

If the exclusive strategy of the church is to add new and different worship services or develop even better marketing campaigns to attract Christians, the church is in trouble.

People aren't flocking to the church like they did in generations past. An increasing number of people simply won't be participating in the established church no matter how excellent the worship services or compelling the programming.

This does not mean the harvest has dried up or people aren't open to things of God. In fact, recent studies seem to point to the exact opposite.[3] I (Jon) have experienced first-hand how God has opened the doors for dozens of spiritual conversations with unchurched friends and neighbors.

However, while an openness to the gospel remains, the church no longer has home field advantage. Our harvesting methods must change. Attractional strategies alone will not reach the growing group of people who are not seeking spiritual answers from the established church.

In his book, *Deep Roots—Wild Branches*, Michael Adam Beck writes, "The inherited church was planted in a different ecosystem . . . and the ecosystem changed, like a desert that swallowed up the jungle. The church in the United States has been through a series of seismic sandstorms . . . and we have failed to adapt . . . while the world has been moving at blazing 5G speeds, we have been stuck on rotary telephones."[4]

Truth be told, the shifts in our culture have been seismic, and the response of the church has been incremental at best.

We must mobilize our missionary disciples to contextualize the gospel for a new frontier. Making disciples in the new frontier will result in new expressions of the church. These pioneering projects are as unique as the individuals God has called. One thing is for sure, making disciples in the 21st-century will require a much greater degree of missional imagination.

We can no longer stay at home waiting for people to flow into our church buildings on Sunday mornings. Instead, we must see ourselves as sent ones and reach our networks, neighborhoods, and third places, where the so-called nones and dones, the unchurched and dechurched, increasingly gather. We are missionaries to a post-Christian culture, not chaplains to Christendom.[5]

Indeed, this new frontier will require a new wave of spiritual entrepreneurs, missionary disciples, innovators, and explorers. We are in desperate need of men and women willing to answer the call to become the pioneering leaders of tomorrow.

This isn't the first time in our history that pioneering leadership was so desperately needed.

We've been here before.

3

THE METHODS OF ASBURY

*Whither am I going? To the New World. What to do?
To gain honor? No, if I know my own heart. To get
money? No: I am going to live to God, and to bring
others so to do.*

Francis Asbury

*Peace be with you! As the Father has sent me,
I am sending you.*

Jesus (John 20:21)

While this may be the first time in our nation's history
that we can speak of our society as post-Christian, in 18th-
century America, the state of Christianity was in similar
decline. In fact, an even smaller percentage of people
attended church then, and most churches felt entirely
irrelevant to the common person.[6]

The culture of the American colonies has often been
romanticized as a city on a hill. While this may have been
the original intent of the Puritans of the 17th-century, by
the late 18th-century, a few decades after the Great
Awakening, the spirituality in the early colonies had
waned.

Perhaps we should take a page out of the playbook of the early American Methodist pioneers who sparked a revival in a culture that, in many ways, parallels the new frontier of the 21st-century.

One of the primary mobilizers of the 18th-century revival in America was a man named Francis Asbury. Asbury lived one of the most remarkable lives in early American history. He was a deeply committed evangelist and apostle, willing to move from the center to the edges of society. If ever there was a pioneering leader, it was Francis Asbury.

Asbury's legacy and life accomplishments, as reported in his journal entries, seem virtually impossible. Through sheer perseverance and dedication to a single goal, he changed the 18th-century religious culture more than any of his contemporaries.

Conservative estimates assert that Asbury traveled over 130,000 miles by horse, crossed the Allegheny Mountains sixty times, visited every state in the Union once a year and rose at 4:00 each morning to spend at least an hour in prayer. Asbury preached more than 10,000 sermons, ordained upwards of 3,000 preachers and was more widely recognized than nearly any person of his generation, including such national figures as Thomas Jefferson and George Washington.[7]

In 1771, when Asbury arrived in the American colonies, there were only four missionaries from England, and America Methodism remained a small handful of congregations from New York to northern Maryland.

The events that unfolded over the next 50 years represent nothing short of a multiplication movement. Consider the following statistics: Between 1771 and 1830, American Methodists achieved a virtual miracle of growth, rising from just a few members to more than 500,000!

When historians consider the larger Methodist influence in America, projections rise as high as 6,000,000 people associated with the movement.[8] At the beginning of the 19th-century, Methodism was exceeding the rate of population growth in every state and major territory in the Union.

In an era where the church was growing increasingly irrelevant, and the nation was expanding westward at a rapid pace, Asbury's default mode was to go with them, and he sent out missionary disciples at every opportunity. In fact, when the early leaders of the movement gathered at the 1790 Conference Asbury explained his plan for the church in this way:

> "Our grand plan, in all its parts, leads to an itinerant ministry. Our bishops are traveling bishops. All the different orders which compose our conferences are employed in the traveling line and our local preachers are, in some degree, traveling preachers. Everything is kept moving as far as possible and we will be bold to say, that, next to the grace of God, there is nothing like this for keeping the whole body alive from the center to the circumference, and for the continual extension of that circumference on every hand."[9]

Asbury's ministry focus was on evangelism, multiplication, and expansion. He was not content to merely "invest and invite" or build brick and mortar churches hoping people would come to him. Instead, he applied persistent pressure to expand the movement from the center to the edges. Asbury would later describe the Methodist movement as "a well-disciplined army" that was primarily comprised of lay people.[10] He understood the importance of raising up pioneering leaders to impact the rapidly changing culture of the new republic.

While Asbury's personal piety, incredible perseverance, and extreme devotion are legendary, it is the army of everyday, pioneering leaders he left in his wake that are more important for us to consider.

So, who were the hundreds and thousands of pioneering leaders in the Methodist movement and what might we be able to learn from them?

4

THE OLD-SCHOOL PIONEERS

The way of the pioneer is always rough.

Harvey S. Firestone

But even if you should suffer for what is right, you are blessed. Do not fear their threats; do not be frightened.

1 Peter 3:14

In 1802, at 26 years of age, Jacob Young took up the challenge of launching a Methodist circuit along the Green River in Kentucky.[11]

Young developed his own strategy for evangelism in the region. He travelled on horseback and stopped every few miles at each settlement to find a family permitting him to preach in their log cabin. Then he went door to door inviting interested friends and family to hear his testimony and the gospel message.

With limited formal education, Young was trained on the job and used his time on horseback for study. His messages were simple, and his focus was always on seeing souls transformed by the power of Christ.

From 1802 to 1803, Young gathered 301 new members and established class meetings wherever he went. For his labors, he received an annual salary of $30, which would have been equivalent to one-tenth of a common laborer.[12]

Clearly, Young's ministry initiative wasn't about the money or fame. Instead, Young's life and ministry were an expression of deep sacrifice and devotion to seeing lost people along the Green River enter the kingdom of God.

Jacob Young reflects the pioneering spirit of the movement. His story could be multiplied hundreds of times over. These early pioneering leaders had a deep commitment to focus on those at the margins of society rather than the center.

Asbury pushed his pioneering leaders to abandon the settled cities and seek a stake in the communities of the back country, including the dangerous and wild frontier.

A growing wave of young and passionate preachers answered the call. One of the early pioneers of the movement shared the following account:

> "We were continually on the lookout for chances to enlarge our work. If we heard of any neighborhood that was destitute of the gospel, we went directly to it and talked with the people; and, if one man in the settlement would open his house for preaching, we made it an appointment, and the next time we came around we were there . . . this is what we mean by a missionary spirit."[13]

These pioneers were missionary disciples and stayed focused on contextualizing the gospel for their generation. They tried to answer the questions of ordinary folk and were considered most successful wherever authority and the social structure were weakest.

People were desperate for a new kind of leadership, represented by common people with a deep love and passion for others and an understandable presentation of the gospel. All these desires were met in the pioneering leaders of the early Methodist movement.

While most of these pioneering leaders had little formal education, they possessed street smarts and quick wit. They had enough education to make them respectable to their listeners, but not so much as to make them appear distant or irrelevant. Their language, humor, sarcasm, and commonsense reasoning appealed to the average person. This allowed them to better contextualize their message.

John Wesley is often recognized for promoting plain truth for plain people. The Methodist movement was a cultural transformation from the grassroots, not a political or ecclesiastical program imposed on the masses from above. It was a groundswell filled with pioneering leaders.

These pioneering leaders were also radically innovative in reaching and organizing people. Long before the rise of church buildings, meetings were typically held in homes, court houses, schoolhouses, barns, and even the open woods.

Methodist itinerant preachers rode their circuits with the belief that bringing the lost to Christ was the highest calling. They assumed their reward would be in heaven and would more than compensate for their suffering on earth.

Indeed, pioneering new faith communities was not an easy life. Pioneering leaders ventured into unknown regions far from family and friends. They were often ridiculed and threatened, and the difficult pace of travel and preaching created the inevitable risk of sickness, accident, and death.

Like many missionary experiences, the tough conditions also created a bond with other traveling preachers. Quarterly gatherings, camp meetings, and annual conferences knit the connection together through a vast network of supportive correspondence.

In the chaos of the late 18th-century, and with religion on the decline, early Methodism adapted and changed to meet the new demands of the time and responded to the cultural shifts with a fresh expression of the church. Onlookers witnessed one of the greatest church planting movements in the history of our nation.

Today, America finds itself in a similar place of social upheaval and in need of a fresh spiritual awakening. The old-world methods are struggling in effectiveness.

What will the future bring?
Will there be an uprising of new pioneering leaders?
Will a new dependence on the Holy Spirit spark a fresh emphasis on the harvest?

5

THE PLENTIFUL HARVEST

*When you're bold, some people will think you're crazy
but it's more insane to be timid.*

Constance Friday

*The harvest is plentiful, but the workers are few. Ask
the Lord of the harvest, therefore, to send out workers
into his harvest field.*

Jesus (Luke 10:2)

There are hundreds and thousands of pioneering leaders living among us, and the number is growing. One of those leaders is Laura.

Although Laura's childhood was filled with pain and brokenness, God redeemed her life. Laura is an incredible woman, and I (Jon) was blessed to have her serve on the team for my second church plant. She is the mother of five children, a hard worker, a faithful wife, and an incredible cook! Comfort food is her specialty, and I was a grateful recipient many times.

A few years into our new church, Laura approached me with a radical sense of calling. In tears, she shared how

God had called her to minister to women trapped in the adult entertainment industry. She had no idea of what steps to take and didn't feel equipped for the task at hand. She only knew most of these women would never step foot in a local church because of their guilt, shame, and fear of being judged. Simply put, she was called to reach a group of people uncomfortable and unfamiliar with the established church.

Not knowing how else to begin, Laura and a friend drove to a notorious strip club one evening and made the decision to sit in the parking lot and pray. This was a habit Laura and her team of prayer warriors would continue for the next few months and soon, they were praying for the bouncers at the door, the club managers, and the patrons. Eventually, the parking lot prayer squad was invited inside of the club and given opportunities to speak with the women.

Through principles we will share in the next few chapters, Laura's team identified needs, started baking cookies and meals for the ladies, explored the faith with them, and soon watched dozens and dozens of people once trapped in an awful industry experience redemption and restoration.[14]

Jesus had a moment with his disciples, where he looked at the surrounding towns and villages and declared, "The harvest is plentiful, but the workers are few. Ask the Lord of the harvest, therefore, to send out workers" (Luke 10:1–2).

The prospect of a plentiful harvest would have sounded exciting to Jesus' disciples, and it should excite us today. It was the incredible harvest that compelled Laura to start her new ministry.

Oddly enough, there are many who look at the post-Christian culture and wonder if the plentiful harvest of Luke 10 is a mere fantasy.

While we may need to change our methods of harvesting, make no mistake about it, the harvest is still plentiful! Even while we rethink our harvesting methods, the local church has an incredible opportunity which ought to create a sense of hope, enthusiasm, and optimism.

The prospect of a plentiful harvest ought to resonate in our hearts like it did for Francis Asbury, Jacob Young, and Laura.

Like Laura discovered, there are certain principles which lead to fruitfulness in ministry. The narrative of Luke 10 provides a fascinating portrayal of how to go about living as a missionary disciple.

Let's get practical and unpack the missionary principles found within Luke's story of Jesus sending out the seventy-two.

6

THE 72

*I will not fear, for you are ever with me, and you will
never leave me to face my perils alone.*

Thomas Merton

*After this the Lord appointed seventy-two others and
sent them two by two ahead of him to every town and
place where he was about to go.*

Luke 10:1

Why did Jesus specifically choose seventy-two people as
pioneering leaders? At first glance, it appears to be a
random number, but what if it was intentional?

The number seventy-two would have recalled a different
narrative about Moses in the book of Numbers. As the
story goes, Moses was trying to lead God's people toward
the Promised Land. At every turn he encountered
complaining, internal pressure, and external struggles. He
was increasingly overwhelmed by the burden of leading
the Hebrew people and found himself frustrated.

There was only one of him and hundreds of thousands of
people he was trying to lead. He couldn't do it alone.
Moses finally reached a breaking point and said to God,
"Why have you brought this trouble on your servant?

What have I done to displease you that you put the burden of all these people on me?" (Num. 11:11).

Moses saw the people as a burden—a bunch of sheep to be shepherded—and he was tired of doing it. He was tired of leading, encouraging, admonishing, deciding, casting vision, and pacifying the grumblers.

In exasperation, Moses finally declared, "I cannot carry all these people by myself; the burden is too heavy for me. If this is how you are going to treat me, please go ahead and kill me" (Num. 11:14–15).

After his trivial death plea, God replied to Moses, "Bring me seventy of Israel's elders who are known to you as leaders and officials among the people. Have them come to the tent of meeting, that they may stand there with you. I will come down and speak with you there, and I will take some of the power of the Spirit that is on you and put it on them. They will share the burden of the people with you so that you will not have to carry it alone" (Num. 11:16–17).

It's good to know God doesn't want us to carry the burdens of the mission alone. In a unique way, God dispersed his authority, the power of his Spirit, and gave it to seventy others. Later in the story, God's power was also released into two other individuals, which is where we find the number seventy-two (Num. 11:26–29).

Moses had a mobilization problem. He needed to engage others to join him in the mission. There were scores of pioneering leaders available, but they hadn't been identified and activated.

The same could be said about many churches today. God has given pastoral leaders an army of men and women to move into the harvest, but they must be identified and activated.

This story of Moses would have come to mind as the early church reflected on the time Jesus sent out the seventy-two. While Jesus didn't share the exasperated emotions of Moses, he did realize the task was too great for any one person to carry. He also knew that one day he would ascend to the Father and would need others to continue the mission. In fact, the sending of the seventy-two comes on the heels of Luke 9:51, where we read, "The time approached for him (Jesus) to be taken up to heaven."

Jesus was looking for workers to carry on the mission. He mobilized a new wave of pioneering leaders to press forward. The focus of the story is on mobilizing pioneering leaders for the harvest. This is not a story about recruiting volunteers for a church program but sending out workers to transform the surrounding towns and villages.

So, who were these seventy-two pioneers?

It is important to note that the seventy-two were volunteers. They had other vocations and weren't considered professional clergy. Luke later tells us they were told not to bring any money along for their ministry. These pioneering leaders took a portion of their time and designated it for the purposes of God. They were individuals who decided to volunteer their hours to help fulfill Jesus' vision.

Origen, an early church father, noted the exact names of each of the seventy-two. If his report is accurate, Luke, a physician and biblical author, was included in the number. Yes, even busy doctors like Luke can be sent out as pioneering leaders.

Interestingly, the first use of the word *sent* in Luke 10 is the Greek word *apostellos*, which is the root word for apostle.

The second Greek word for *send* used in this passage is *ekballo,* which means to compel one to depart. The use of this word is couched in what appears to be stern language. It means casting out with force. There is nothing passive about being a sent one. We *must* go!

As we go, Luke mentions Jesus sent his disciples *two by two*. In the same way, the pioneering leaders of today will be wise to not go-it-alone.

Doing ministry with others is a value of pioneering leadership. In fact, a good first step in pursuing pioneering leadership is to pray for a partner. In partnership, there is increased accountability, support, witness, camaraderie, and power. This might look like a husband and wife team, two friends working together, or it might mean a few associates.

Make no mistake about it, as we'll see in the rest of the Luke 10 story, moving into the harvest field can be hard and we'll need somebody to lean on.

7

THE INSTRUCTIONS

Catch on fire and people will come for miles to watch you burn.

John Wesley

Go! I am sending you out like lambs among wolves. Do not take a purse or bag or sandals; and do not greet anyone on the road.

Luke 10:3–4

BE COURAGEOUS

The pioneering leaders of days gone by are often described as adventurous, hardened, aggressive types with a rigid exterior and a battle-tested persona. However, when Jesus described the seventy-two, he used the metaphor of being *like a lamb*.

The imagery of a lamb is a striking contradiction to our preconceived ideas about the rugged pioneer, but it needs to be considered. Lambs are simple and without defense. While the calling is one of adventure and risk, the posture needs to be one of humble submission to the Good Shepherd. There are dangers, to be sure, but we must rely on God and God alone to be our defense.

Indeed, Jesus' seventy-two, his first pioneering leaders, might have appeared weak to some, but their simple words and unarmed presence were part of their attraction and appeal.

With God's missional assignments, there will always be wolves and opposition. There will be those in the world hostile to the message of the gospel. There will be those in the church thinking you are foolish or unwise for associating with lost people in the places they gather. There might even be those who try to compromise the group you are gathering.

Wolves can come in a variety of ways, which is yet another reason Jesus tells us to minister in pairs. Don't give up because of opposition or rejection. Rather, expect it. Don't be surprised when an explanation of your work is met by blank stares. Innocent lambs wandering into a wolf pack should not expect to come out unscathed.

Be courageous and trust God as you go.

BE FLEXIBLE

Pioneering leaders must also be flexible. In the first-century, most people preparing for a journey would pack an extra pair of sandals in case the first pair wore out.

However, Jesus didn't want his pioneering leaders bringing a bunch of supplies, a big suitcase, bulky bags, extra sandals, or anything else causing them to be inflexible. Jesus' bias was toward action and being flexible along the way.

When you meet a group of people and enter your mission field, assume the Holy Spirit has already gone ahead of you. Assume God is working on the people in the community and simply ask if someone might open their home to you. Talk to them about Jesus, and then eat whatever they feed you.

There is an underlying principle here of flexibility and being led by the Spirit. Living the life of a pioneering leader is less about developing a ministry action plan in your personal war room and more about getting out into the community to see where Jesus is already working. This method requires dependence on God, Spirit-led leadership, and a high degree of flexibility.

BE FOCUSED

Within the first-century culture, it was common for a conversation along the road to last for hours on end. Hospitality was a core virtue of the time, and people were expected to fulfill the unwritten rules of society.

Interestingly, Jesus mentioned this dynamic, and told the seventy-two to not get involved in long, complicated, unnecessary conversations. The point being, don't get side-tracked and be sure to remain focused on the mission.

If God has called you to reach your neighborhood for Christ, you may need to say *no* to the other relationships pulling you away from what God has called you to do.

Don't spend too much time hanging out with those who are getting you sidetracked. Stay focused on who God has called you to reach.

Jesus was known as *a friend of sinners* because he prioritized attending broken people's social gatherings and events. Jesus came to seek and save the lost and didn't have time to consume all the religious events of his day. Jesus' interactions were purposeful and focused.

In the same way, if you lack clarity of missional purpose, you may get sucked into meaningless activities (even church-sponsored activities) and lose sight of the harvest. As we are sent out, we must stay focused and say *yes* only to those things contributing to the harvest.

Luke reminds us, reaching lost people should always be our end goal. As we go into the harvest fields, we must be *courageous*, *flexible*, and *focused*. However, we must also have a process for engaging the people God has called us to reach. Let's continue to explore the instructions of Christ in Luke 10.

8

THE PROCESS

Peace begins with a smile.

Mother Teresa

When you enter a house, first say, "Peace to this house." If someone who promotes peace is there, your peace will rest on them; if not, it will return to you. Stay there, eating and drinking whatever they give you, for the worker deserves his wages. Do not move around from house to house. When you enter a town and are welcomed, eat what is offered to you. Heal the sick who are there and tell them, "The kingdom of God has come near to you."

Luke 10:5-9

BRING A BLESSING

Whoever God has called you to reach and wherever he asks you to go, enter as a humble lamb and bring a blessing of peace.

Pioneering leaders spread the peace of Christ and bring people together. They don't barge in and brashly announce the message of the gospel. When they go to work, school, the grocery store, or even as they walk around the neighborhood, they are quick to remember their call is to always be a blessing and prepare the way for the gospel with kindness and peace.

It's interesting to note, Jesus didn't ask the seventy-two to proclaim the gospel message when they first entered the town. Jesus called them to bring peace. Even more, Jesus directed them to private houses rather than to the marketplace or the public arena.

When speaking to the twelve disciples Jesus said, "Search there for some worthy person and stay at their house until you leave" (Matthew 10:11b). This mode of operation is important to consider. We are to bring a blessing of peace, look for people of peace, and attempt to bring relationships together.

If God has called you to pioneer a new work, be sure to bring a blessing and search out a person of peace. If someone only wants to argue or seems to bring division, show them love but then move on to actively seek out those who will receive your peace offering.

BUILD RELATIONSHIPS

By now, you understand the wisdom of finding a partner in ministry and a person of peace, which will lead to more connections. The temptation will often be to rush forward too quickly and start gathering people in a formalized group. Perhaps a better next step is to deepen relationships.

Showing love to others is spelled T-I-M-E. We need to be willing to invest time. Jesus told his pioneers, "Stay there, eating and drinking whatever they give you . . . do not move around from house to house" (Luke 10:7).

Can you hear Jesus' voice? Stay there. Invest time. Be a blessing. Lead with peace. Build strong relationships and eat good food together!

BEGIN TO MEET NEEDS

In the context of relationships and in the course of conversation, you will be made aware of the needs of individuals. We live in a broken world and everyone has struggles. People struggle with addiction, depression, divorce, hurting friendships, loved ones with cancer, loss of employment, or a host of other things in life.

Jesus said it this way, "Heal the sick who are there and tell them, 'The kingdom of God has come near to you'" (Luke 10:9). If someone is sick, pray for them and ask God to demonstrate his power. If someone can't find a job, pray for them and ask God to help them find employment. If someone is depressed, pray for a spirit of joy. If someone is dabbling in witchcraft or pagan practices, let them know there is someone named Jesus who loves them. Pray for their healing and wholeness in this life.

Notice, in Luke 10:9, Jesus mentioned physical healing first and gospel proclamation second. Often, the meeting of physical needs or healing paves the way for spiritual breakthrough and acceptance of God's inner transformation.

Keep in mind, meeting physical needs and praying for others is essential, but the greatest need people have is for a lifelong relationship with their Savior.

Meeting felt needs simply allows people to see the power of love and the power of God. When people experience God's power it takes less convincing for them to accept Jesus as Lord and Savior.

9

THE P.I.O.N.E.E.R.

It is not easy to be a pioneer, but oh, it is fascinating! I would not trade one moment, even the worst moment, for all the riches in the world.

Elizabeth Blackwell

Have faith in God . . . Truly, I tell you, if anyone says to this mountain, "Go, throw yourself into the sea," and does not doubt in their heart but believes that what they say will happen, it will be done for them.

Jesus (Mark 11:22–23)

The blueprint of Luke 10:1-9 has served as a backdrop for the work of pioneering leaders. To make it even more memorable, we've designed a simple and practical acrostic of the word PIONEER to illustrate these principles. Consider using the following prompts as a starting point for launching a new pioneering project:

- **P**ray
- **I**nvest
- **O**bserve
- **N**eeds
- **E**at
- **E**xplore
- **R**edeem

PRAY

In Luke 10:2, Jesus said, "Ask the Lord of the harvest . . . to send out workers." Prayer is the first step in this process. Pioneering is not something to be taken lightly. Pioneering can be dangerous work at times, and we are sent as *lambs among wolves*. This danger requires courage, and as we engage those uncomfortable or unfamiliar with the established church, we must begin with prayer and fasting.

Pray for God to speak clearly to you and show you where you are called to go and who you are called to reach. Pray for courage and wisdom and ask God for direction.

INVEST

While prayer will continue throughout the process, the next step is to make an investment in the people you hope to serve. Establish a few initial relationships with people in the community that you feel called to reach.

If your zone of impact is a neighborhood, start hanging out at the local park or community center. If it is a specific coffee shop, begin to invest time there getting to know the workers and patrons.

Discern your calling through prayer and fasting and then ramp up your investment with your specific group. Offer the gift of presence and be sure to spend extra time getting to know the people you will soon serve.

OBSERVE

The investment of time will no doubt yield a few key observations. What have you noticed about the environment? What are the main topics of conversation? Who are you beginning to meet? Are there any people of peace you can identify? How can you be a blessing to this group of people? What are some of the existing needs? Are there any tangible ways you can serve?

During the observation phase of pioneering you are asking God to show you a path forward and seeking to discern how to move from simply investing time to meeting needs.

NEEDS

Meeting people's needs ought to happen naturally. After prayer and investment, you will begin to make observations and discern ways you can meet tangible needs.

Perhaps the easiest way to move into a conversation on meeting needs is to ask the simple question, "How can I pray for you?" Even in the most post-Christian context, this prayer-oriented question will often be received well and provide insight into the spiritual temperature of a person. It will also show you some next steps in how to pray, give, love, serve, or go.

Be sure to share with others how they can pray for you as well. Allowing others to serve your needs is a great step forward as Jesus encouraged the seventy-two to *eat and drink whatever* they offer you. This posture of humility will often build deeper connections.

EAT

Jesus did most of his ministry around tables. Eating is a great way to begin to move from individual conversations to the formation of community.

Remember, you have hopefully started this pioneering project with someone else and moved quickly toward finding your person of peace, the natural bridge-builder in the community.

Sharing a meal could look like a dinner at home, an outdoor grill-out, restaurant visit, progressive party, dessert night, or coffee outing. The objective of any pioneering project is to begin to form a community of faith. A meal is one of the best ways for community to form. Consider making a shared meal an ongoing function of the group.

EXPLORE

Notice in this process, you have prayed, invested, observed, met needs, and connected over a shared meal. Now it is time to explore the faith.

Begin to discern whether the group would like to explore spiritual topics, engage the stories of Jesus, pray, or serve others outside of the group. Introduce a brief devotion, offer meaningful questions for discussion, or simply read a section of Scripture.

It's possible that after sharing a few meals together, spiritual topics have already been discussed. Or, perhaps two or three individuals have begun to express interest in spiritual things. At this point, you simply need to draw the net and set a date to meet again.

Either way, the goal at this stage is to begin to introduce prayer, Scripture, and opportunities to serve others within the daily rhythms of the group.

REDEEM

Finally, as you continue to build relationships and explore the faith, God will start to transform hearts and allow you the opportunity to see people cross the line of faith and be redeemed.

Building relationships with others and helping them learn how to trust and follow Jesus is the process of disciple making. This is the pivotal step where people are brought from death to life and put their trust in Jesus. This is what it's all about!

PUTTING IT ALL TOGETHER

If we were to put this entire seven-step process together it might look something like this storyline:

You and your spouse feel called to pioneer a new work in your neighborhood and you spend a few weeks in *PRAYER* and fasting, asking God to guide you in the right direction. You sense God is asking you to invite one other couple to join you in the initial effort, and the four of you begin to have regular times in prayer.

You begin by *INVESTING* in a handful of families that God has drawn you to and start spending extra time talking at the local playground with your kids. Investing in these relationships is a priority. You try to get to the park at least four or five times a week and regularly hang out in your front yard initiating conversations.

During this period of relationship building, you *OBSERVE* a half dozen families living in your neighborhood and you realize they are not very connected in the community. Additionally, one of the dads is going through a nasty divorce and a few others are struggling at work.

You decide one way to meet these *NEEDS* is to ask individuals how you can be praying for them. God is using this compassion and concern to help you build a specific bridge with one of the couples eager for new friendships. They also seem to be a person of peace, as they are the natural glue for other relationships. You and the other family invite them over for dinner. The six of you enjoy learning more about each other's stories and you even have an opportunity to share your testimony of when you crossed the line of faith in your own life.

A month later, all six of you decide to host a grill-out in your backyard on a Friday night. After all, everyone likes to *EAT!* Four of the five families on your list respond to the invitation and you encourage them to bring a part of the meal. You open the mealtime with a very brief prayer, and by the end of the evening ask if they would like to rotate homes on a regular basis and have a meal once a month.

Six months into this process, you begin to *EXPLORE* where people are at in their relationship with God and a few jump at the opportunity to explore their spirituality further. You do this by meeting every other Thursday night for a quick meal, reading a chapter of the Bible together, and offering prayer requests.

There are now eight of you meeting every Thursday, and the men and women also decide to meet outside of the group for discipleship and accountability. Through a memorable spiritual conversation, the neighbor going through a divorce is *REDEEMED* and finds new life in Christ! Praise God! This redemption story is celebrated at your next meeting.

Congratulations! You are now the pioneer of a new faith community, and God is confirming his calling on your life. Perhaps, this new community of faith will continue to grow and expand as you are faithful to live out the principles of Luke 10.

CONCLUSION

ARE YOU A PIONEERING LEADER?

"It is not the critic who counts; not the man who points out how the strong man stumbles, or where the doer of deeds could have done them better. The credit belongs to the man who is actually in the arena, whose face is marred by dust and sweat and blood."

Theodore Roosevelt

Pioneering leaders are *missionary disciples called to find creative ways to engage and serve a group of people uncomfortable or unfamiliar with the established church.*

Who are these pioneering leaders?

It might be you.

Pioneering leaders come from every walk of life. They are entrepreneurs, homemakers, construction workers, teachers, baristas, and dozens of other co-vocational leaders who have each been given a specific people group to reach and a mission to accomplish.

Many of these pioneering leaders will launch vibrant outreach ministries and initiatives within the context of their local churches. Perhaps a local church has an entire division and network of pioneering leaders extending the message of the gospel outside the walls of the church.

Other pioneers will start these projects only to find them bubble up into something they would have never first imagined. Like many of the original seventy-two, these pioneers will discover a deeper calling they didn't know existed and become church planters, future micro-church network leaders, and movement makers.

Either way, it is our conviction these pioneering leaders will create a groundswell, ultimately ushering in a kingdom tide of new churches designed to change the culture and impact the new frontier of the 21st-century.

If you are a pastor leading a local congregation, then you have a handful, a dozen, or perhaps hundreds of pioneering leaders waiting to be mobilized. The harvesting methods are changing, and you can multiply your influence by establishing a vast network of pioneering leaders and micro-church planters. Everyone has the potential to be a missionary disciple.

In fact, one author writes, "We believe people need to see the church less as something someone else starts and runs that we choose to consume, to believing the church can be something like a family that each of us pursues and engages."[15]

The ultimate mission is to make disciples from the harvest. When the mission is being faithfully lived out, churches will naturally emerge.

Does this mean every pioneering leader will ultimately plant a church? Not necessarily. Many pioneering leaders will remain tethered to an established church and receive training, community, and other resources from the inherited congregation.

For many, this arrangement will be a beautiful picture of renewal, a give and take relationship. One author likens this paradigm to a giant tree with deep roots (the established church) and wild branches (the pioneering projects).[16]

Nevertheless, many pioneering leaders will be called to launch new autonomous churches and transition from a missionary disciple to a church planter. In fact, for those interested in learning more about this transition, we have included a short appendix with some helpful thoughts on what we call an essential ecclesiology.

Here are a few questions you might ask yourself as you discern whether or not God is calling you to be a pioneering leader:

- Are you called to reach a specific group for Christ?
- Are you a self-starter and motivated to move forward?
- Do you regularly look for practical ways to get things done?
- Can you rally others to join you on projects?
- Are you persistent and resilient?
- Can you bring people together and are you good at building community?
- Are you able to discern and meet needs?
- Can you live with a certain degree of flexibility and are you able to think outside the box?
- Would you describe yourself as spiritually healthy?

There is one final point at the end of Luke 10 we want you to see, and it's a beautiful picture of what can happen when men and women step out in faith.

As expected, the seventy-two eventually returned to Jesus. They had prayed, invested, observed, met needs, ate with others, explored the faith, and saw physical and spiritual healing. People were redeemed, spiritual strongholds were broken, and there was a palpable enthusiasm as they returned to share their experiences with Christ.

The seventy-two returned with joy and said, "Lord, even the demons submit to us in your name." Jesus replied, "I saw Satan fall like lightning from heaven. I have given you authority to trample on snakes and scorpions and to overcome all the power of the enemy; nothing will harm you. However, do not rejoice that the spirits submit to you, but rejoice that your names are written in heaven" (Luke 10:17–20).

In a spontaneous moment, Jesus prayed, "I praise you, Father, Lord of heaven and earth, because you have hidden these things from the wise and learned, and revealed them to little children. Yes, Father, for this is what you were pleased to do." Then he turned to his disciples and said privately, "Blessed are the eyes that *see what you see*. For I tell you that many prophets and kings wanted *to see what you see* but did not see it, and to hear what you hear but did not hear it" (Luke 10:21–24; emphasis added).

Do you see it?

The harvest is plentiful.

The opportunities are everywhere.

Jesus is with us.

Will you be counted as a courageous pioneer?

If God is calling you to pioneer a new work in your community or if you would like to learn more about mobilizing the pioneering leaders in your church, please visit:

www.groundswellmovement.net

APPENDIX

WHAT'S A CHURCH?

DEFINING YOUR ESSENTIAL ECCLESIOLOGY

Many pioneering leaders will eventually need to wrestle with an important question. How do we describe this new gathering of people? There are some projects that will remain outreach ministries in established churches; others will evolve into a missional community or small group; and for some, the real possibility exists of becoming a new church.

Today, there are a variety of different names given to these churches. They are called microchurches, fresh expressions, house churches, and even outposts. However, what is required for a pioneering project to become a healthy church?

Becoming a new church, formed primarily from discipling relationships, stirs up questions of ecclesiology. *Essential ecclesiology* is a phrase given to the necessary ingredients for a church to operate in its most primitive expression.

One author says it this way, "The essential ecclesiology is the starting point of the church, not the end. It is meant not as a license to underachieve, but as the beginning of a sense of ownership of the church by all."[17]

If the definition of church is too complicated, we will unknowingly eliminate scores of capable church planters and missionary disciples. Conversely, if the definition of the church is too bare, then we may negatively affect future generations.

Here's the tension.

Imagine the earlier example about the pioneering project in the neighborhood, many of whom met at the local park. The local park is not a church when those families first begin to meet. If you determine to gather on a Sunday morning at the park to play with your kids, drink coffee, and engage in conversation, the local park is still not a church.

However, what happens when your time together begins to include prayer? What if a few of those people give their life to Christ through other activities happening during the week? What if your group begins to make sacrifices for one another and begins to share their testimony with others? What if they commit to gathering at the park every week at 10:00 a.m.?

When does this group of people become a church?

This type of scenario is why we need to have clarity on our essential ecclesiology. While everyone may have a slightly modified description, working through the question, "What is a church?" is critical.

The early church adopted the word *ecclesia* from Greek culture and used it to describe their newly forming faith communities. *Ecclesia*, in English, can be rendered *the called-out-ones.* These three words can be useful to help give categories for describing a good framework for the church.[18]

First, is the word *called.* Those who are called have surrendered to the Lordship of Christ and are following Jesus. Simply put, they are disciples of Christ. Worship is ultimately about surrender, not only singing or reciting a specific liturgy. It is the devotion of the community to Jesus as Lord and offering themselves as living sacrifices. The church must be gathered around the resurrected Christ.

Second, is the word *out.* The church not only gathers around the authority of Christ but is also sent out to those unaware of his love and grace. Mission is about making disciples and engaging with those who don't know Jesus. The Great Commission is the starting point, and the church is the vehicle for its accomplishment. Mission is not something we add to our churches—it is the core of the church. One author writes, "Church exists by mission, just as a fire exists by burning. Where there is no mission, there is no church."[19]

Third, is the word *ones.* The church is understood to be a covenant community of baptized believers. Community is about the relationships emerging between those living under the same Lordship in the presence of his Spirit. To paraphrase a common definition of many microchurches, "The church is a worshipping community on mission."[20] Our common submission to Christ and engagement in mission forms the community resulting in a church.

While the definition, "A worshipping community on mission," may appear truncated to many, it provides a starting point for further elaboration. Here are a few other questions which may crop up in your context as you think biblically and historically about the church.

- What about biblically qualified leadership?
- What about the sacraments of the Lord's Supper and baptism?
- What about church discipline and authority?
- How is right doctrine preserved?
- How often should the church meet?
- How many people are required?

We believe any essential ecclesiology should begin by processing these seven words:

- Worship
- Community
- Mission
- Leadership
- Sacraments
- Discipline
- Doctrine

Helping pioneering leaders know when their project becomes a church is an important part of the process.

ENDNOTES

1. Collins, T (2015). *Fresh Expressions of Church.* Franklin, TN: Seedbed. p.2.

2. Richardson, R (2019). *You Found Me. New Research on How Unchurched Nones, Millennials, and Irreligious Are Surprisingly Open to Christian Faith.* Downers Grove, IL: IVP. p.7.

3. http://www.billygrahamcenter.com/youfoundme/resources/

4. Beck, M. (2015). *Deep Roots, Wild Branches: Revitalizing the Church in the Blended Ecology.* Franklin, TN: Seedbed. p.22

5. Collins, T (2016). *From the Steeple to the Street: Innovating Mission and Ministry Through Fresh Expressions of Church.* Franklin, TN: Seedbed. p.8.

6. Wood, G (2009). *Empire of Liberty: A History of the Early Republic, 1789-1815.* New York, NY: Oxford University Press. p.581.

7. Wigger, J. (2009). *American Saint: Francis Asbury and the Methodists.* New York, NY: Oxford University Press. p.3

8. Addison, S. (2011). *Movements that change the world: Five keys to spreading the gospel:* Downers Grove, IL. IVP Press. p.87.

9. Wigger, J. (1998). *Taking heaven by storm: Methodism and the rise of popular Christianity in America.* New York, NY: Oxford University Press. p.33.

10. Hatch, N. (1989). *Democratization of American Christianity.* New Haven, CT: Yale University Press. p.86.

11. Addison (2011), p.88.

12. Wright, C. (1889). *Comparative wages, prices and the cost of living.* Boston, MA: Wright and Potter Printing. p.48

13. Richey, R. (2015). *Methodism in the American Forest.* New York, NY: Oxford University Press. p.32.

14. See www.jerichooutreachministry.org for more information.

15. Sanders, B. (2019). *Microchurches.* Tampa, FL: Underground Publishing. p.20.

16. Beck, M.

17. Sanders, (2019). p.35

18. https://www.wesleyan.org/whats-a-church

19. Collins, T. (2018). p. 109.

20. Sanders, B (2019). p.34.

www.ingramcontent.com/pod-product-compliance
Lightning Source LLC
Chambersburg PA
CBHW030405160726
47992CB00007B/2966